The Winding Journey

A road unending...

Yashna Shah

BookLeaf
Publishing

India | USA | UK

Made with ❤ on the BookLeaf Publishing Platform
www.bookleafpub.in
www.bookleafpub.com

Dedication

For those who listen to their hearts.

For the dreamers who see the world through words.

And for the quiet moments that inspired every line...

Preface

Every poem in this book began as a quiet thought, a fleeting emotion, or a moment that stayed with me longer than I expected. Writing them was a way to understand life, to make sense of feelings, and to hold onto experiences that might otherwise pass unnoticed.

The Winding Journey: A Road Unending is about movement — not just the steps we take in the world, but the inner journeys of the heart and mind. Some poems explore hope, some pain, some the small joys that can go unseen, but each one reflects a part of the path I've walked, and the path we all share in some way.

I hope that as you read these verses, you'll find pieces of your own story within them. That perhaps they will make you pause, reflect, connect and see your own journey a little more clearly.

Thank you for walking this road with me.

— *Yashna Shah*

Acknowledgements

To mom and dad who provided me with the first
audience for my poems.
To Shruti miss and Malben sir for their constant
guidance and encouragement.

This would not have been possible without you.

Across the table with Him: Understanding the Almighty

A place like Eden, where motives speak
Determining your life, aflame or bleak.

Whispering silence, a peek inside
Poking pain, but riddance alike.

Majestically royal, fantasy drips
An attempt of yours, the rest will be His.

Friend, companion, idol or love
World of affection, tranquil dove.

Just acceptance' what's needed with all your heart
To make Him: the master of your life
The reign - holder of your cart.

An Unbreakable Spirit

Falling back is not an option
Dignity and chance are laid as auction
With every bit of sand that falls
A bit of you is forever lost.

An aim to live the life manifested
Shall be washed away like a plant not rooted
The roots your morals, the soil your firmness
On which depends your life of an empress.

Be willing to walk alone
For many who started with you,
Shall not stay until you're rotten and gone.

Rigidity & flexibility share a meaning of their own
Controversial use, a sign of vigour torn.

A major lesson in life to learn
To face life's reality,
In times of mourn.

Honesty – convenience; a game of choice
A powerful reply for those
Who dare to voice.

A Healing Embrace

Is forgiveness an option?
Oh! Such a hypothetical question.
If to forgive is a choice,
Will moving on ever live a voice?

In a world where cruelty's at its peak,
Whispers of falsehood, all around us speak,
Wreck and roar making the headline,
Human existence paid as a fine.

"Live in the present" — sounds so free,
Forgetting the past — a cause for glee.
What is it that scares us true,
Keeping us away from peace' view?

Forgiveness is nothing less than magic,
Letting you off from this world so tragic.
Just wait and watch; it'll do its work —
The result of honour, your patience' worth.

Live a life that's grand and new,
For forgiveness is not an option —
It's *nature's cue.*

Ashes of the Past

My life seems lost, my heart seems torn.
Life has lost its meaning—
Or have I lost it all?

There are four stages of pain, and I have it all in my shell.
But I'd like to add one more: Revenge—against myself.

They say: there's nothing worse than a chance not taken.
Today, with the experience of this, I stand fully
awakened.

But what use is this realization?
After missing the train, what use is standing at the
station?

Remorse and regret have filled me to the brim,
An invisible scar, far beyond my skin.
A mistake so great, an act so massive
Smile on the face, but tears on the passive.

Forgiving before being sorry is the greatest virtue of all,
But introspection of the opposite is a sign of the fall.
The greatest virtue becomes the greatest sin
If you don't have the courage to accept—for your own
well-being.

An Unchained Heart

She walked through the streets alone,
Having ice cream, shake, and scone,
Enjoying life the way it was,
Without chasing friends or laws.

She had understood what life meant:
Faking happiness is not how it's dealt.
Acceptance is power, failure is grace;
Success is from within, not on the face.

Now the dependence is gone—she rests in peace,
Known to life's mystery, succeeding at ease.

She can now truly feel herself,
The way she had never before,
She was now beyond the boundary of —
The basic mist of flesh and bone.

She felt awakened from a long sleep
Of pain, remorse, revenge, and weep.

She answered the call that came from within,
And recognized it as her own skin.

She found solace in that one voice,
That gave her strength
To always make the right choice.

The Forgiven Flame

A city with prosperity at its peak,
Where houses were of gold, where bronze seemed bleak.
No beggar, not a single thief,
Ecstasy in the air, no place for grief.

But a black magic was cast overnight;
The colours soon changed—
From merry music to shrieks of fright.

Everything destroyed, leaving a memory of the past—
Who knew how long even that would last?

Some suggested that it was a curse indeed,
Others said that it was envy's weed.
No one knew the true reason,
That it was neither resent nor treason.

The seed had been sown long back
By a man whom the city once backed—

A gem, he was once called as
Who knew that behind this was the mind of that lad's?

A genius, now a destructive mastermind,
The hands which once carved breakthroughs
Now this mayhem designed.

But he too was bound by pledge tense,
Given by his ancestors, which made the scene intense.
He was driven by a passion wild,
Worse than heroin, compelled to abide.

The people, when found that it was him in reality,
They dropped their weapons and took on a guise of
tranquility.
They welcomed him with warm grace;
They knew the heart underneath that rigid face.

The man was shattered,
His teeth clattered.
He thanked them for a new chance,
And paused a moment, as if held in a trance.

He had understood the meaning of real victory,
Understood love—and the rest is history.

The Last Sunrise: First Peace

Death has always been cold and tense,
But what if it's only a pretence?
What if death gifts us freedom
From this world, so gruesome?

Death has always meant a boundary to life,
But what if I tell you there is a meaning to 'strife'?
The soul is the one to merge and join,
But do you have the courage to flip the coin?

There is an opening at every close;
Is there a better way to defeat the inner woes?
Let's greet death like an old friend,
For its certainty is far from being held.

The mystery of death yet remains to be sought
By those who dare to terminate their fraught.
Remember, the path ahead is easy nigh,
For at every step, the stakes are high.

The Twin Shadows of Silence:
When alone is a choice,
When alone is a sentence...

It is said by people oft,
Solitaire is for the soft.
A boon for introverts, it's called,
Before societal norms did crawl.

Today I make an announcement wild,
To crush the deluded beliefs of the mild.
Solitaire is a choice that demands nerve,
Valour and silence it does serve.

Another word as well today hovers my brain,
With solitaire, it's often related.
I beg distinction, not without reason,
Today I declare an open act of confession.

Seclusion too is disconnection from the rest,
But tears and stifling are often buried within the crest.
Self-choice is the one separating the two:
One—a call for peace; other—bringing in the sadness crew.

Same situation but varied feelings; such is the cryptic maze of life:
One, a garland of flowers; other, a fatal knife.

Fractured Bonds

Friends—a boon, a curse, or both,
For whom does our heart bleed,
With love or loath?
Love! A common answer I hear,
But at the core, it's wrong—I fear.

My heart has been shred into pieces two,
Broken eternally, impossible to renew.
But here I stand in confusion wild,
Which part to obey—the massive or the mild?

One asks to rejoice when foes depart,
Other whispers forgiveness from the heart.
I don't find a reason to reject either,
Hunting for a way to obey neither.

Let's step out in search of an answer true,
Towards ourselves and a world anew.
First—why do we need a companion at all?
Just to drape around a cosy shawl?

Satisfaction can be found from within as well,
Just don't let your self-respect melt.
Today I stand alone, yet powerful;
The land is barren, yet so beautiful...

When the School Bell rings...

The last day has finally arrived,
Flooding my mind with memories wild.
I remember my cries to avoid school,
And now these thoughts blur my view.

I remember the corridors hogged during break,
Shouts that followed, yet makes me shake.
Races wild in the hallway—
Here was the birth of the bathroom Coldplay.

The first handshake, the final goodbye,
The coaster of friendship, low and high.
I still remember the ringing laughter,
And also the lunch breaks' hungry banter.

School teachers to professors,
A transition steep and coarse.
Finally, we move forward today,
Life's greater battles pave our way.

A thread entangled, unable to loosen,
Emotions intense, unable to reason.
I lack courage to pull myself together,
A piece of me shall maybe stay stuck forever.

When the Last Bell rings...

Finally, it's time to depart—
Friends, scoldings, tiffin tart.
Memories are not proving enough
To sail me through days—smooth and rough.

Memories will be the only takeaway;
This grieving thought makes my soul fray.
A decade long has been spent amidst these walls—
With detentions, laughter, chats, and brawls.

These huge gates shall never be crossed again,
A reflection appalling, driving me insane.
I'd made my peace with memories, though—
Like a sea unlevel, through which you row.

But apparently the oars are proving ponderous,
Sabotaging survival against the sea so perilous.
I would like a chance to relive my life,
And prepare myself for this tedious strife.

Unheard Echoes

Anger brewing, warm and high,
She let it out with a cold sigh.
She felt unheard, day and night,
And craved a shoulder after every fight.

But a flaw internal she bore,
That made her *own* heart sore.
Unaware of it, she carried on,
The heavy baggage through each new dawn.

External foes were all she knew,
Blind to the strength within her too.
Her restless mind began to tire,
Extinguishing peace, inflaming fire.

She was unaware of her true friends,
Who persisted through all her mental trends.
They loved her without a cost,
Even when her sanity was lost.

Constant nagging was all she could hear;
Who could help, when her sight was unclear?
But soon the veil of truth was swept,
Feeling overwhelmed, she wept.

She felt regret, a stern sensation,
But faults and breaks always birth a new creation.
The hard core of misconception had finally melted,
The massive mountain had finally been defeated.

The Trend of Approval

Pleasing people has become the trend,
An endless habit we struggle to mend.
Self-understanding fades away,
While prying in others is the norm today.

There was a time when our friends were the stars,
The moon, the sky, the universe was ours.
Now the days are gone, the joy is lost.
The world's undergone a revolution for a twinge of frost.

The world's unaware that it is merely for a while,
A ray of light and it will run a mile.
Fake things are temporary, don't sink lower;
Be a trendsetter, and not a mere follower.

The Shift

I drowned myself in self-fury,
Non-conducive to be my own jury.
I experienced a deep sense of rejection—
Wildness amusing lay, since it was my own sanction.

A fact so grave I discerned that night,
As I lay, sanity drifting away from my sight:
There is light as long as your eyes are unlatched;
A mere distortion makes the universe seem patched.

This daunting fact creeps over every palm,
Through every clenched fist, shaking the calm.
Fire of passion, the zeal of ambition—
The noise and quiet meet at this station.

The fear of losing the noise,
The terror of forever poise—
This is what ruins the balance of self,
Like a cloud overshadowing your inner realm.

Converting pity of self into mercy for rest
Is what puts your endurance to test.
Your present can be a dream for someone else—
Make it a place where joy undoubtedly dwells.

For—what esteem does a free result carry?
Make your draft sterner,
'Stead of praying the sea to be merry.

Northern Star

Sailing through life with grace and ease,
With a smile that brings all to their knees.

A heart so pure, a soul so bright,
The world is blessed with your shining light.

In all you do, you bring such sight,
Painting our minds with colours bright.

Teacher—a word with synonyms so many:
Philosopher, guide, a friend uncanny.

Blessed are those who have a beacon like you,
And in this world, distinct are those few.

Maze of Mirrors

I looked around, far and wide,
Tossing my glance from side to side.
A piece of land with people strange,
Who, *in view*, were out of my range.

But our view of things is often deceptive;
It varies with a change in perspective.
The changes visible scared me to the core,
And opened to me an unknown door.

The people around me were weird in a way,
Intensely different as night and day.
They had an identity of two faces,
One of which was available for the masses.

This is the one which we often know of,
As sweet, adorable, tender, and soft.
However, the other one is terrifying as hell,
Yet unaware, it keeps us well.

As I walked over to the back,
Forced my eyes into the sack,
The sight within left me in fathom,
Of truth, which until now felt so random.

Two cruel eyes glaring at me,
A smile sarcastic, chiding me.
Its hands wrapped around my neck,
Draining blood with a sharp peck.

Pain of a torment I could feel,
As the wicked hands dragged me in,
Into a maze so delusional,
Recovery became a hope irrational.

Today I muse over a solemn thought:
Why has the world chosen to rot?
No one seems to wish for true joy,
Others' feelings have conveniently become a toy.

Texts and Truths

Today I talk about two such words,
Who carve the niche of the universe.
They emerge from the same womb,
Together compose the soul's bloom.

Literacy and wisdom are those terms,
One lights the lamp, while the other burns.
A thin line separates the two;
Not everyone can get the clue.

Literacy is the result of hard work,
Wisdom is patience's perk.
One stays confined to a shelf of books,
Other roams, through hills and brooks.

Literacy is ink wrapped in fortune,
Wisdom speaks the universe's tune.
Letters fade with time's lore,
Lessons grow in tempest's core.

Education dissipated from understanding
Is like a ripe fruit left hanging.
It has fortune without a doubt,
Yet *value* it keeps well out.

Seek to be learned, for it carries honour
Learn to be silent, for it carries a new flavour.
In a world shouting and craving attention,
Your silence will be seen as a peaceful intervention.

Throne of Thorns

When I look around the revolving world,
Blending together, crafting a cult,
Passion such I view from a distance,
Fearing the fire, dreading the brunt.

I find my aloof closure safe,
To resist the impending chafe,
Yet I remain apprehensive of the fact,
That the world shall render the pact.

I was promised that I'd be left alone,
Their hearts, however, are carved of stone.
I hope my closure's not taken over,
By the expanding empire of plastic flower.

This era, however, cannot be trusted;
The broken will sure leave you busted.
Your honour is at the mercy of you,
To protect it is the game of none but few.

The cocoon of illusion can leave you in awe,
It's nothing but the infusion of a new flaw.
Remain earthed in this world, striving to reach the sky,
For it's the soil that bore your every silent cry.

When the Universe Revolts

You've patched me up in pieces so many,
Shattering me with deceit and vanity.
I gave you thought to make you divine,
Not to make you doubt the design.

You've made me a pawn of your master game,
Dictating my moves like an animal tame.
But unaware you are of the immense power,
The supremacy that can avenge you by slaughter.

The creator is the caster of the spell,
He is the one, however, buried within the shell.
But the creation, when it hurts his pride,
A destruction mammoth shall bestride.

Humility transforms itself into revenge;
Blood shall drain from the body that feared a scratch.
Don't mistake my silence for weakness,
It's the quieter one who always bears the harness.

You carved your glory upon my face;
Begun by you, I'll end the chase.
I bear a dominion greater than all machinery;
In my fury will burn all your arms and cavalry.

Acknowledge my presence, and you'll be grateful;
Don't wage a war that can leave you regretful.
A warning it is from the universe's end,
Broken are your ways, crucial to mend.

For I rise unbound, no chains remain;
Your throne shall crumble under my reign.

Melodies of the Golden Age

Before pixels painted our skies,
An era with which we've severed ties.
I depict a time of joy so effortless,
When rose beds and lilies us did caress.

An era when friendships meant no pretence,
When petals filled our souls with pure fragrance.
Peace was seen as a graceful ornament,
Worn on eyes, carrying a powerful sentiment.

Joy was found in Sunday shows,
Duck tales were the sweetest dose.
Knocking on doors without a cause,
And holding back to take a pause.

A voice that held hearts captive,
A sensation which was too addictive.
Though the mic is silent, his voice still rings
Ameen Sayani yet remains, the king of the radio kings.

A silent wish to revive those days,
A quiet longing for olden ways.
Remain alive as a spark in those
Who have known a life of complete repose.

The Winding Journey

I woke up today, fat and flustered,
Droopy eyes, dreams all clustered.
I was a girl so careless;
Life was but a game, tactless.

Wandering idly through roads and streets,
I came upon a café serving treats.
I went in and sat by the window,
When an unexpected visitor's voice did echo.

I looked up to see a woman, regal,
Her gaze as sharp as the soaring eagle.
Poised and pretty, she offered her hand,
Befriending me with grace so grand.

She sat down facing me.
Bewildered, I smiled meekly.
I mused why an angelic beauty as her
Would talk to me, making my heart stir.

We started to converse, slow but bright.
Minutes passed by, out of my sight.
It wasn't long before I noticed a connection,
A stiffer bond that broke the tension.

It was as if we were the same soul,
Sharing thoughts, ideologies, and every goal.
But her presence was more pronounced than mine,
Leaving me silent, caught in her shine.

She soon uncovered her true identity,
Revealing to me our shared affinity.
She said that she was the *future me*,
Someone I would grow up to be.

She spoke to me about the truths of life,
Explained to me the importance of strife.
Time is treasure, ought to be saved;
Education is wealth, ought to be craved.

An advice profound that changed my life,
Cut through my cons as a sharp knife.
It made me worthy of glorious success,
Protecting me from external menace.

That one conversation with the future me
Expanded my view and set me free.

I boldly embraced the *Winding Journey*
To the future self I was meant to be.